BOOK OF MORMON
for
Young Readers
JOURNAL

By Kelli Coughanour

point
PUBLISHING

This Journal
Belongs To:

Brenda Jane

Worsham

If lost go to this adress:
1679 Milford way
92223

Beaumont, CA

Published by Point Publishing
Copyright 2015

Check out www.BookofMormonforYoungReaders.com

Cover and title page images by Briana Shawcroft. Full images can be found in *The Book of Mormon for Young Readers*

All layout and interior design graphics by Hannah Ungricht Design

ISBN 978-0-9962729-0-2

Printed in the United States of America
Liberty Press, Springville, UT

> "Get a notebook, a journal that will last through all time, and maybe the angels may quote from it for eternity. Begin today and write in it."
> *- President Spencer W. Kimball*

This journal is a companion to *The Book of Mormon for Young Readers* and provides an easy way for you to write about and remember important and meaningful things as you study. Add to your journal each time you read (there are extra pages at the back if you need more room to write!). Notice how applying what you learn blesses your life. Come to the scriptures each day prepared to learn and looking to be taught by the Spirit.

Whether this is your first time reading through the scriptures, or one of many times, recorded thoughts and feelings can become a treasure for a lifetime!

Journal + Share:

Write down anything that you learned, or want to know more about, or any special feelings you have. It would be great to share what you wrote with your parents!

Date 5/30/18

What do you learn from this story that can help you in your life?

It can I

Continued on page 1

What will you do today to be better at following what the prophet counsels

us to do? Write how this makes you feel.

Continued on page 1

What thoughts, feelings, or questions do you have from this story?_____

What is your favorite scripture from this story? How does it help you? _____

_____

_____

_____

_____

_____

_____

_____

_____

_____

_____

_____

_____

_____

_____

_____

_____

_____

_____

MEMORIZE

Can you say the Memorize verse when you only see the first letter of each word?

"I_____ a_ Y_ S____ K___ M_ C_____. Y_ S____ P_____."

(1 NEPHI 2:20)

Draw or doodle about any impressions you had as you read or anything that stood out to you from this story:

Word cloud fun! Write words in the cloud that help you remember important things from this chapter:

See page 18 from the Book for an example.

Date _____

What do you learn from Nephi's faith that can help you? _____

_____

_____

_____

_____

_____

_____

_____

Continued on page _____

What will you begin to do today to help you have an "I Will Do" attitude

like Nephi? Write how this affects you. _____

_____

_____

_____

_____

_____

Continued on page _____

What thoughts, feelings, or questions do you have from this story?_____

_____

_____

_____

_____

_____

_____

_____

_____

_____

_____

_____

_____

_____

_____

_____

_____

_____

_____

What is your favorite scripture from this story? How does it help you? _____

_____

_____

_____

_____

_____

_____

_____

_____

_____

_____

_____

_____

_____

_____

_____

_____

_____

MEMORIZE

Can you say the Memorize verse when you only see the first letter of each word?

"I W___ G_ a__ D_ T__ T_____ W____ T__ L___ H___ C_____."
(1 NEPHI 3:7)

Draw or doodle about any impressions you had as you read or anything that stood out to you from this story:

Word cloud fun! Write words in the cloud that help you remember important things from this chapter:

Date _____

What can you learn from this story about handling difficult

things in your life? _____

_____

_____

_____

_____

_____

_____

_____

Continued on page _____

What will you do each day to have your prayers be more meaningful to you?

Write how this makes a difference. _____

_____

_____

_____

_____

_____

_____

Continued on page _____

What thoughts, feelings, or questions do you have from this story? _____

What is your favorite scripture from this story? How does it help you? _____

_____

_____

_____

_____

_____

_____

_____

_____

_____

_____

_____

_____

_____

_____

_____

Can you say the Memorize
verse when you only see
the first letter of each word?

MEMORIZE

"T__ L___ I_ a___ T_ D_ a__
T_____ a_____ T_ H__ W___."
(1 NEPHI 7:12)

Draw or doodle about any impressions you had as you read or anything that stood out to you from this story:

Word cloud fun! Write words in the cloud that help you remember important things from this chapter:

See page 18 from the Book for an example

Date _____

What do you learn from this story about how you can better

understand and learn God's teachings? _____

_____

_____

_____

_____

_____

_____

_____

Continued on page _____

Write things you will do to show your faith in God, then record how these

choices affect you. _____

_____

_____

_____

_____

_____

Continued on page _____

What thoughts, feelings, or questions do you have from this story?_____

_____

_____

_____

_____

_____

_____

_____

_____

_____

_____

_____

_____

_____

_____

_____

_____

_____

_____

What is your favorite scripture from this story? How does it help you? _____

_____

_____

_____

_____

_____

_____

_____

_____

_____

_____

_____

_____

_____

_____

_____

_____

Can you say the Memorize
verse when you only see
the first letter of each word?

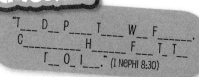

MEMORIZE

"T___ D__ P____ T____ W__ F_____.
C_____ H_____ F___ T_ T__
Г__ O_ I___." (1 NePHI 8:30)

Draw or doodle about any impressions you had as you read or anything that stood out to you from this story:

Word cloud fun! Write words in the cloud that help you remember important things from this chapter:

Date _____

What do you learn from Nephi's example for solving problems

that can help you? _____

_____

_____

_____

_____

_____

_____

_____

Continued on page _____

What will you do differently today to become better at following the Spirit?

Write how this helps you. _____

_____

_____

_____

_____

_____

_____

Continued on page _____

What thoughts, feelings, or questions do you have from this story?_____

_____

_____

_____

_____

_____

_____

_____

_____

_____

_____

_____

_____

_____

_____

_____

_____

_____

What is your favorite scripture from this story? How does it help you? _____

_____

_____

_____

_____

_____

_____

_____

_____

_____

_____

_____

_____

_____

_____

_____

_____

_____

Can you say the Memorize
verse when you only see
the first letter of each word?

MEMORIZE

"B_ S____ M____ T__ L___ C__
B____ a____ G____ T____."
(1 Nephi 16:29)

Draw or doodle about any impressions you had as you read or anything that stood out to you from this story:

Word cloud fun! Write words in the cloud that help you remember important things from this chapter:

See page 18 from the Book for an example

Date _____

What do you learn from Nephi about accomplishing new or challenging things? _____

_____

_____

_____

_____

_____

_____

_____

Continued on page _____

What will you work on today that might be hard, but important, for you to do? Write how this affects your life. _____

_____

_____

_____

_____

_____

_____

Continued on page _____

What thoughts, feelings, or questions do you have from this story? _____

What is your favorite scripture from this story? How does it help you? _____

_____

_____

_____

_____

_____

_____

_____

_____

_____

_____

_____

_____

_____

_____

_____

_____

_____

MEMORIZE

Can you say the Memorize verse when you only see the first letter of each word?

"I_ G__ H__ C_____ M_ T_
D_ a__ T_____ I C____ D_ T___."
(I Nephi 17:50)

Draw or doodle about any impressions you had as you read or anything that stood out to you from this story:

Word cloud fun! Write words in the cloud that help you remember important things from this chapter:

Date _____

What can you learn from this story about how your choices

affect other people? _____

_____

_____

_____

_____

_____

_____

Continued on page _____

Write one thing you will start doing to become more like Jesus Christ, then

record how this makes you feel. _____

_____

_____

_____

_____

_____

Continued on page _____

What thoughts, feelings, or questions do you have from this story?

What is your favorite scripture from this story? How does it help you? _____

_____

_____

_____

_____

_____

_____

_____

_____

_____

_____

_____

_____

_____

_____

_____

MEMORIZE

Can you say the Memorize
verse when you only see
the first letter of each word?

"I D__ L____ a__ S_____ U___
U_. T___ I_ M____ B_ F__ O__ P____
a__ L_____." (1 NePHI 19:23)

Draw or doodle about any impressions you had as you read or anything that stood out to you from this story:

Word cloud fun! Write words in the cloud that help you remember important things from this chapter:

See page 18 from the Book for an example

Date _____

What can you learn from Nephi that will help you in your life?

_____

_____

_____

_____

_____

_____

_____

_____

Continued on page _____

What will you do today to have greater happiness in your own family? Write

how this makes a difference in your family. _____

_____

_____

_____

_____

_____

_____

Continued on page _____

What thoughts, feelings, or questions do you have from this story? _____

What is your favorite scripture from this story? How does it help you? _____

_____

_____

_____

_____

_____

_____

_____

_____

_____

_____

_____

_____

_____

_____

_____

_____

Can you say the Memorize
verse when you only see
the first letter of each word?

MEMORIZE

"a___ F___ T___ M_ M___ B_:
a__ M__ a__, T___ T__ M____
H___ J__." (2 NePHI 2:25)

Draw or doodle about any impressions you had as you read or anything that stood out to you from this story:

Word cloud fun! Write words in the cloud that help you remember important things from this chapter:

Date _____

What do you learn from Jacob about how to stay strong in your faith? _____

_____

_____

_____

_____

_____

_____

Continued on page _____

What will you do each day to help you live the gospel in any situation?

Write how this affects you. _____

_____

_____

_____

_____

_____

Continued on page _____

What thoughts, feelings, or questions do you have from this story?_____

_____

_____

_____

_____

_____

_____

_____

_____

_____

_____

_____

_____

_____

_____

_____

_____

_____

What is your favorite scripture from this story? How does it help you? _____

_____

_____

_____

_____

_____

_____

_____

_____

_____

_____

_____

_____

_____

_____

_____

_____

_____

_____

MEMORIZE

Can you say the Memorize
verse when you only see
the first letter of each word?

"S___ N__ T_ C_____ T__ L___,
B__ T_ T___ C_____ F___
H__ H___." (JACOB 4:10)

Draw or doodle about any impressions you had as you read or anything that stood out to you from this story:

Word cloud fun! Write words in the cloud that help you remember important things from this chapter:

See page 18 from the Book for an example

Date _____

What do you learn from Enos about repenting? _____

_____

_____

_____

_____

_____

_____

Continued on page _____

Write what you will do to improve your prayers so you can feel closer to

Heavenly Father and His love. Record how this makes you feel. _____

_____

_____

_____

_____

_____

_____

Continued on page _____

What thoughts, feelings, or questions do you have from this story?_____

_____

_____

_____

_____

_____

_____

_____

_____

_____

_____

_____

_____

_____

_____

_____

_____

_____

What is your favorite scripture from this story? How does it help you? _____

_____

_____

_____

_____

_____

_____

_____

_____

_____

_____

_____

_____

_____

_____

_____

Can you say the Memorize
verse when you only see
the first letter of each word?

MEMORIZE

"T__ F____ H___
M___ T___ W____."
(ENOS 1:8)

Draw or doodle about any impressions you had as you read or anything that stood out to you from this story:

Word cloud fun! Write words in the cloud that help you remember important things from this chapter:

Date _____

What can you learn from this story about the importance of

keeping a journal? _____

_____

_____

_____

_____

_____

_____

Continued on page _____

What will you do today to show you are trying to do what God wants you to

do? Write how this affects you. _____

_____

_____

_____

_____

_____

Continued on page _____

What thoughts, feelings, or questions do you have from this story?_____

What is your favorite scripture from this story? How does it help you? _____

_____

_____

_____

_____

_____

_____

_____

_____

_____

_____

_____

_____

_____

_____

_____

_____

_____

Can you say the Memorize verse when you only see the first letter of each word?

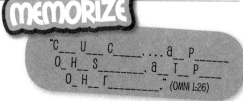

MEMORIZE

"C___ U___ C____. . . . a__ p_____
O_ H__ S_____, a__ T__ p____
O_ H__ r_____." (OMNI 1:26)

Draw or doodle about any impressions you had as you read or anything that stood out to you from this story:

Word cloud fun! Write words in the cloud that help you remember important things from this chapter:

See page 18 from the Book for an example

Date _____

What truth did King Benjamin teach that you loved, and why

do you love it? _____

_____

_____

_____

_____

_____

_____

Continued on page _____

Think of ways you will serve others, then write them down so you remember!

Record how serving makes you feel. _____

_____

_____

_____

_____

_____

_____

_____

Continued on page _____

What thoughts, feelings, or questions do you have from this story? _____

_____

_____

_____

_____

_____

_____

_____

_____

_____

_____

_____

_____

_____

_____

_____

_____

_____

What is your favorite scripture from this story? How does it help you? _____

_____

_____

_____

_____

_____

_____

_____

_____

_____

_____

_____

_____

_____

_____

_____

Can you say the Memorize
verse when you only see
the first letter of each word?

MEMORIZE

"W___ Y_ a__ I_ T__ S_____ 0_
Y___ F_____ B_____ Y_ a__ 0___ I_
T__ S_____ 0_ Y___ G__." (MOSIAH 2:17)

Draw or doodle about any impressions you had as you read or anything that stood out to you from this story:

Word cloud fun! Write words in the cloud that help you remember important things from this chapter:

Date _____

What do you learn about choices from this story? _____

_____

_____

_____

_____

_____

_____

_____

Continued on page _____

Write what you will do to make good decisions in your life, then share about

times when these things help you. _____

_____

_____

_____

_____

_____

_____

Continued on page _____

What thoughts, feelings, or questions do you have from this story? _____

_____

_____

_____

_____

_____

_____

_____

_____

_____

_____

_____

_____

_____

_____

_____

_____

_____

What is your favorite scripture from this story? How does it help you? _____

_____

_____

_____

_____

_____

_____

_____

_____

_____

_____

_____

_____

_____

_____

_____

MEMORIZE

Can you say the Memorize
verse when you only see
the first letter of each word?

"W___ I_ T__ W___
O_ T__ L___."
(MOSIAH 6:6)

Draw or doodle about any impressions you had as you read or anything that stood out to you from this story:

Word cloud fun! Write words in the cloud that help you remember important things from this chapter:

See page 18 from the Book for an example

Date _____

What can you learn from Abinadi and Alma that will help you

in your life? _____

_____

_____

_____

_____

_____

Continued on page _____

How can you prepare so you can talk about the gospel with confidence like

Abinadi? Share about times when this helps you. _____

_____

_____

_____

_____

_____

_____

Continued on page _____

What thoughts, feelings, or questions do you have from this story?_____

What is your favorite scripture from this story? How does it help you? _____

_____

_____

_____

_____

_____

_____

_____

_____

_____

_____

_____

_____

_____

_____

_____

_____

MEMORIZE

Can you say the Memorize verse when you only see the first letter of each word?

"L___ M_ a__
K___ M_ C_____."
(MOSIAH 13:14)

Draw or doodle about any impressions you had as you read or anything that stood out to you from this story:

Word cloud fun! Write words in the cloud that help you remember important things from this chapter:

Date _____

How have you or your family been blessed by doing what the prophet asks you to do? _____

_____

_____

_____

_____

_____

_____

Continued on page _____

What will you do today to show love and kindness to others? Record how doing this affects you. _____

_____

_____

_____

_____

_____

Continued on page _____

What thoughts, feelings, or questions do you have from this story?_____

What is your favorite scripture from this story? How does it help you? _____

_____

_____

_____

_____

_____

_____

_____

_____

_____

_____

_____

_____

_____

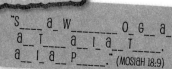

Can you say the Memorize verse when you only see the first letter of each word?

"S____ a_ W_____ O_ G__ a_ a__ T____ a__ I_ a__ T_____, a__ I_ a_ P_____." (MOSIAH 18:9)

Draw or doodle about any impressions you had as you read or anything that stood out to you from this story:

Word cloud fun! Write words in the cloud that help you remember important things from this chapter:

See page 18 from the Book for an example

Date _____

How have difficult things in your life made you a stronger

person? _____

_____

_____

_____

_____

_____

_____

Continued on page _____

What will you do to have a good attitude even when something doesn't go

how you want it to? Write how this makes a difference. _____

_____

_____

_____

_____

_____

_____

_____

Continued on page _____

What thoughts, feelings, or questions do you have from this story?_____

_____

_____

_____

_____

_____

_____

_____

_____

_____

_____

_____

_____

_____

_____

_____

_____

_____

_____

What is your favorite scripture from this story? How does it help you? _____

_____

_____

_____

_____

_____

_____

_____

_____

_____

_____

_____

_____

_____

_____

_____

_____

MEMORIZE

Can you say the Memorize verse when you only see the first letter of each word?

"S_____ C_____ a__ W___ P_____ T_ a__ T__ W___ O_ T__ L___." (MOSIAH 24:15)

Draw or doodle about any impressions you had as you read or anything that stood out to you from this story:

Word cloud fun! Write words in the cloud that help you remember important things from this chapter:

Date _____

What do you learn from this story about the affects of

repenting? _____

_____

_____

_____

_____

_____

_____

Continued on page _____

What will you do differently to better feel the blessings of forgiveness?

Record how this affects you. _____

_____

_____

_____

_____

_____

Continued on page _____

What thoughts, feelings, or questions do you have from this story?_____

What is your favorite scripture from this story? How does it help you? _____

_____

_____

_____

_____

_____

_____

_____

_____

_____

_____

_____

_____

_____

_____

_____

MEMORIZE

Can you say the Memorize verse when you only see the first letter of each word?

"a_ O____ a_ M_ P____
r_____ W___ I F_____ T___."
(MOSIAH 26:30)

Draw or doodle about any impressions you had as you read or anything that stood out to you from this story:

Word cloud fun! Write words in the cloud that help you remember important things from this chapter:

See page 18 from the Book for an example

Date _____

How can the sons of Mosiah inspire you to make good use of your time each day? _____

_____

_____

_____

_____

_____

_____

Continued on page _____

Write what you will do today to put God first in your life, then share how this makes you feel. _____

_____

_____

_____

_____

_____

Continued on page _____

What thoughts, feelings, or questions do you have from this story? _____

What is your favorite scripture from this story? How does it help you? _____

_____

_____

_____

_____

_____

_____

_____

_____

_____

_____

_____

_____

_____

_____

MEMORIZE

Can you say the Memorize
verse when you only see
the first letter of each word?

"W___ I_ T__
W___ O_ T__ L___."
(MOSIAH 29:43)

Draw or doodle about any impressions you had as you read or anything that stood out to you from this story:

Word cloud fun! Write words in the cloud that help you remember important things from this chapter:

Date _____

What do you learn from Nehor about the danger of really

seeking popularity? _____

_____

_____

_____

_____

_____

_____

_____

Continued on page _____

What will you do to make sure you are following God's plan for you? Write

how this helps you. _____

_____

_____

_____

_____

_____

Continued on page _____

What thoughts, feelings, or questions do you have from this story?_____

_____

_____

_____

_____

_____

_____

_____

_____

_____

_____

_____

_____

_____

_____

_____

_____

_____

_____

What is your favorite scripture from this story? How does it help you? _____

_____

_____

_____

_____

_____

_____

_____

_____

_____

_____

_____

_____

_____

_____

_____

Can you say the Memorize verse when you only see the first letter of each word?

MEMORIZE

"[B_] S_____ a__ l_____
l_ K_____ T_ C_____
O_ G___." (alma 1:25)

Draw or doodle about any impressions you had as you read or anything that stood out to you from this story:

Word cloud fun! Write words in the cloud that help you remember important things from this chapter:

See page 18 from the Book for an example

Date _____

What can you do to follow Alma's example and stand against

bad things going on in our day? _____

_____

_____

_____

_____

_____

_____

Continued on page _____

What will you do today to strengthen your faith in prayer? Record how doing

this makes a difference. _____

_____

_____

_____

_____

_____

Continued on page _____

What thoughts, feelings, or questions do you have from this story? _____

_____

_____

_____

_____

_____

_____

_____

_____

_____

_____

_____

_____

_____

_____

_____

_____

What is your favorite scripture from this story? How does it help you? _____

_____

_____

_____

_____

_____

_____

_____

_____

_____

_____

_____

_____

_____

_____

MEMORIZE

Can you say the Memorize
verse when you only see
the first letter of each word?

"T__ L___ D__ H___ T____
C____. a__ D__ S_____
T___." (alma 2:28)

Draw or doodle about any impressions you had as you read or anything that stood out to you from this story:

Word cloud fun! Write words in the cloud that help you remember important things from this chapter:

Date _____

Which of Alma's questions means the most to you, and why is it meaningful? _____

_____

_____

_____

_____

_____

_____

_____

Continued on page _____

What will you do today to fill your heart with more of the love of God and a

greater desire to be like Jesus? _____

_____

_____

_____

_____

_____

Continued on page _____

What thoughts, feelings, or questions do you have from this story?

What is your favorite scripture from this story? How does it help you? _____

_____

_____

_____

_____

_____

_____

_____

_____

_____

_____

_____

_____

_____

_____

MEMORIZE

Can you say the Memorize
verse when you only see
the first letter of each word?

"T____ I_ T__
T__ a__ L____ G__."
(alma 5:13)

Draw or doodle about any impressions you had as you read or anything that stood out to you from this story:

Word cloud fun! Write words in the cloud that help you remember important things from this chapter:

See page 18 from the Book for an example

Date _____

What can you do to keep your thoughts appropriate and good?

_____

_____

_____

_____

_____

_____

Continued on page _____

What will you do in your life to show you care more about living the gospel

of Jesus Christ than anything else? Write how doing this makes you feel.

_____

_____

_____

_____

_____

_____

Continued on page _____

What thoughts, feelings, or questions do you have from this story?_____

_____

_____

_____

_____

_____

_____

_____

_____

_____

_____

_____

_____

_____

_____

_____

_____

_____

_____

What is your favorite scripture from this story? How does it help you? _____

_____

_____

_____

_____

_____

_____

_____

_____

_____

_____

_____

_____

_____

_____

_____

_____

_____

_____

MEMORIZE

Can you say the Memorize
verse when you only see
the first letter of each word?

"T__ L___ H__ G_____ U__ T___
P____, a_____ T.T____ F____
W____ W__ I_ C_____." (alma 14:28)

Draw or doodle about any impressions you had as you read or anything that stood out to you from this story:

Word cloud fun! Write words in the cloud that help you remember important things from this chapter:

Date _____

What are ways you can help the Lord bless others? _____

_____

_____

_____

_____

_____

_____

_____

Continued on page _____

What will you do differently to be more reliable and dependable like

Ammon? Write how this choice blesses you. _____

_____

_____

_____

_____

_____

_____

Continued on page _____

What thoughts, feelings, or questions do you have from this story? _____

What is your favorite scripture from this story? How does it help you? _____

_____

_____

_____

_____

_____

_____

_____

_____

_____

_____

_____

_____

_____

_____

_____

Can you say the Memorize
verse when you only see
the first letter of each word?

MEMORIZE

"[G___] S_____ I_
T__ K_____ O_ T__ T____."
(alma 17:2)

Draw or doodle about any impressions you had as you read or anything that stood out to you from this story:

Word cloud fun! Write words in the cloud that help you remember important things from this chapter:

Date _____

What do you learn from Ammon about how to help others to

want to learn more about Jesus Christ? _____

_____

_____

_____

_____

_____

_____

Continued on page _____

How will you show that you love and believe in Jesus Christ? Write how

doing these things makes you feel. _____

_____

_____

_____

_____

_____

Continued on page _____

What thoughts, feelings, or questions do you have from this story?_____

_____

_____

_____

_____

_____

_____

_____

_____

_____

_____

_____

_____

_____

_____

_____

_____

_____

_____

_____

What is your favorite scripture from this story? How does it help you? _____

_____

_____

_____

_____

_____

_____

_____

_____

_____

_____

_____

_____

_____

_____

_____

_____

MEMORIZE

Can you say the Memorize verse when you only see the first letter of each word?

"T____ H_____ H__ B___ C_____:
T___ T___ H__ N_ M___ D_____
T_ D_ e___." (alma 19:33)

Draw or doodle about any impressions you had as you read or anything that stood out to you from this story:

Word cloud fun! Write words in the cloud that help you remember important things from this chapter:

Date _____

What can you learn from this story about standing up for

what you know is right? _____

_____

_____

_____

_____

_____

_____

Continued on page _____

What things will you do today to help you listen to and follow the Holy Ghost

even better? Share about times when you know He helps you. _____

_____

_____

_____

_____

_____

_____

_____

Continued on page _____

What thoughts, feelings, or questions do you have from this story?

What is your favorite scripture from this story? How does it help you? _____

_____

_____

_____

_____

_____

_____

_____

_____

_____

_____

_____

_____

_____

Can you say the Memorize
verse when you only see
the first letter of each word?

MEMORIZE

"I_ T__ S_____ O_ T__ L___
T__ [C__] D_ a__ T_____."
(aLMa 20:4)

Draw or doodle about any impressions you had as you read or anything that stood out to you from this story:

Word cloud fun! Write words in the cloud that help you remember important things from this chapter:

See page 18 from the Book for an example.

Date _____

Describe a time when you made a choice that showed your

faith in Jesus Christ. _____

_____

_____

_____

_____

_____

_____

Continued on page _____

What is something you will stop doing today so you can be more obedient to

what Jesus wants you to do? Write how this change makes you feel. _____

_____

_____

_____

_____

_____

_____

Continued on page _____

What thoughts, feelings, or questions do you have from this story?_____

_____

_____

_____

_____

_____

_____

_____

_____

_____

_____

_____

_____

_____

_____

_____

_____

What is your favorite scripture from this story? How does it help you? _____

_____

_____

_____

_____

_____

_____

_____

_____

_____

_____

_____

_____

_____

_____

_____

Can you say the Memorize
verse when you only see
the first letter of each word?

MEMORIZE

"I_ H__ S_____ I
C__ D_ a__ T_____."
(alma 26:12)

Draw or doodle about any impressions you had as you read or anything that stood out to you from this story:

Word cloud fun! Write words in the cloud that help you remember important things from this chapter:

Date _____

Korihor at first claimed he didn't believe in God. When have you felt like God knows and loves you? _____

_____

_____

_____

_____

_____

_____

Continued on page _____

What will you do differently to show you are trying to be like Jesus Christ?

Write how doing this affects you. _____

_____

_____

_____

_____

_____

Continued on page _____

What thoughts, feelings, or questions do you have from this story? _____

_____

_____

_____

_____

_____

_____

_____

_____

_____

_____

_____

_____

_____

_____

_____

_____

_____

_____

What is your favorite scripture from this story? How does it help you? _____

_____

_____

_____

_____

_____

_____

_____

_____

_____

_____

_____

_____

_____

_____

_____

MEMORIZE

Can you say the Memorize
verse when you only see
the first letter of each word?

"C_____ Y_ T__ D__;
W__ Y_ W__ S____."
(Alma 30:8)

Draw or doodle about any impressions you had as you read or anything that stood out to you from this story:

Word cloud fun! Write words in the cloud that help you remember important things from this chapter:

Date _____

What have you felt or experienced that has helped your

testimony to grow? (Be patient if you're still working on having a testimony.)

_____

_____

_____

_____

_____

_____

_____

Continued on page _____

What is one thing you will do today to strengthen your faith in Jesus Christ?

Write how this makes a difference. _____

_____

_____

_____

_____

_____

_____

Continued on page _____

What thoughts, feelings, or questions do you have from this story?_____

_____

_____

_____

_____

_____

_____

_____

_____

_____

_____

_____

_____

_____

_____

_____

_____

_____

What is your favorite scripture from this story? How does it help you? _____

_____

_____

_____

_____

_____

_____

_____

_____

_____

_____

_____

_____

_____

_____

_____

_____

MEMORIZE

Can you say the Memorize verse when you only see the first letter of each word?

"F____ I_ N__ T_ H___ a P_____ K_____ O_ T_____: ... I_ Y_ H__ F____ Y_ H___ F__ T____ W___ a__ N__ S__, W___ a_ T___." (aLMa 32:21)

Draw or doodle about any impressions you had as you read or anything that stood out to you from this story:

Word cloud fun! Write words in the cloud that help you remember important things from this chapter:

Date _____

What are ways you will protect yourself against the bad

temptations in our world? _____

_____

_____

_____

_____

_____

_____

_____

Continued on page _____

Write down choices you will make in your life that will help you return

home to God. _____

_____

_____

_____

_____

_____

_____

Continued on page _____

What thoughts, feelings, or questions do you have from this story? _____

_____

_____

_____

_____

_____

_____

_____

_____

_____

_____

_____

_____

_____

_____

_____

_____

What is your favorite scripture from this story? How does it help you? _____

_____

_____

_____

_____

_____

_____

_____

_____

_____

_____

_____

_____

_____

_____

_____

Can you say the Memorize
verse when you only see
the first letter of each word?

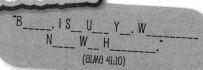

MEMORIZE

"B_____, I S__ U___ Y__ W_____
N____ W__ H_____."
(alma 41:10)

Draw or doodle about any impressions you had as you read or anything that stood out to you from this story:

Word cloud fun! Write words in the cloud that help you remember important things from this chapter:

See page 18 from the Book for an example

Date _____

God helped the Nephites accomplish their righteous goals.

What is a goal you have that you can pray for help with?_____

_____

_____

_____

_____

_____

_____

_____

Continued on page _____

What will you do to receive the blessings of being faithful to God?_____

_____

_____

_____

_____

_____

_____

_____

_____

Continued on page _____

What thoughts, feelings, or questions do you have from this story?_____

What is your favorite scripture from this story? How does it help you? _____

_____

_____

_____

_____

_____

_____

_____

_____

_____

_____

_____

_____

_____

_____

_____

_____

Can you say the Memorize
verse when you only see
the first letter of each word?

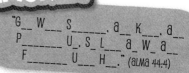

MEMORIZE

"G__ W___ S_____, a__ k___, a__
P_____ U_, s_ l___ a_ w_ a__
F_____ U___ H__." (alma 44:4)

Draw or doodle about any impressions you had as you read or anything that stood out to you from this story:

Word cloud fun! Write words in the cloud that help you remember important things from this chapter:

Date _____

What do you learn from this story about the importance of covenants? _____

_____

_____

_____

_____

_____

_____

_____

Continued on page _____

Write what you will do today to be a good influence on those you're around.

Record how doing this makes you feel. _____

_____

_____

_____

_____

_____

_____

Continued on page _____

What thoughts, feelings, or questions do you have from this story?_____

LIBERTY

What is your favorite scripture from this story? How does it help you? _____

_____

_____

_____

_____

_____

_____

_____

_____

_____

_____

_____

_____

_____

_____

_____

_____

MEMORIZE

Can you say the Memorize
verse when you only see
the first letter of each word?

"C___ F____ I_ T__
S_____ O_ T__ L___."
(alma 46:20)

Draw or doodle about any impressions you had as you read or anything that stood out to you from this story:

Word cloud fun! Write words in the cloud that help you remember important things from this chapter:

See page 18 from the Book for an example

Date _____

What in your life has been a weakness, but with your work

and God's help has become easier? _____

_____

_____

_____

_____

_____

_____

Continued on page _____

What are qualities that Captian Moroni had that you might want too? How

could having these help you? _____

_____

_____

_____

_____

_____

_____

_____

Continued on page _____

What thoughts, feelings, or questions do you have from this story? _____

_____

_____

_____

_____

_____

_____

_____

_____

_____

_____

_____

_____

_____

_____

_____

_____

What is your favorite scripture from this story? How does it help you? _____

_____

_____

_____

_____

_____

_____

_____

_____

_____

_____

_____

_____

_____

_____

_____

_____

_____

MEMORIZE

Can you say the Memorize
verse when you only see
the first letter of each word?

"T____ W__ W___ F_____
I_ K_____ T__ C_____
O_ T__ L___ W___ D_____
a_ a__ T____." (alma 50:22)

Draw or doodle about any impressions you had as you read or anything that stood out to you from this story:

Word cloud fun! Write words in the cloud that help you remember important things from this chapter:

Date _____

Fighting among the Nephites destroyed their peace. How can you bring more happiness and unity into your family? _____

_____

_____

_____

_____

_____

_____

_____

Continued on page _____

What distraction will you work on today so you can focus more on the important things in your life? Write how making this change helps you. _____

_____

_____

_____

_____

_____

Continued on page _____

What thoughts, feelings, or questions do you have from this story? _____

_____

_____

_____

_____

_____

_____

_____

_____

_____

_____

_____

_____

_____

_____

_____

_____

What is your favorite scripture from this story? How does it help you? _____

_____

_____

_____

_____

_____

_____

_____

_____

_____

_____

_____

_____

_____

_____

_____

MEMORIZE

Can you say the Memorize verse when you only see the first letter of each word?

"T___ W___ . . . T___ a_ a__ T____
I_ W_____ T____ T___ W___
e_____." (alma 53:20)

Draw or doodle about any impressions you had as you read or anything that stood out to you from this story:

Word cloud fun! Write words in the cloud that help you remember important things from this chapter:

See page 18 from the Book for an example

Date _____

Why were ALL of the 2000 stripling warriors saved? _____

_____

_____

_____

_____

_____

_____

Continued on page _____

What are ways you can follow God's teachings with exactness so you can be

protected like the stripling warriors? _____

_____

_____

_____

_____

_____

_____

Continued on page _____

What thoughts, feelings, or questions do you have from this story?

What is your favorite scripture from this story? How does it help you? _____

_____

_____

_____

_____

_____

_____

_____

_____

_____

_____

_____

_____

_____

_____

_____

_____

Can you say the Memorize
verse when you only see
the first letter of each word?

MEMORIZE

"I_ T___ D__ N__ D____.
G__ W____ D_____ T___."
(alma 56:47)

Draw or doodle about any impressions you had as you read or anything that stood out to you from this story:

Word cloud fun! Write words in the cloud that help you remember important things from this chapter:

Date _____

When was a time that having a positive attitude helped you?

_____

_____

_____

_____

_____

_____

Continued on page _____

What will you do each day to stay faithful to God even when you go

through hard things? Write how this helps you. _____

_____

_____

_____

_____

_____

_____

Continued on page _____

What thoughts, feelings, or questions do you have from this story?_____

What is your favorite scripture from this story? How does it help you? _____

_____

_____

_____

_____

_____

_____

_____

_____

_____

_____

_____

_____

_____

MEMORIZE

Can you say the Memorize
verse when you only see
the first letter of each word?

"G_ F____ ... I_ T__
S_____ O_ T__ L___."
(alma 61:18)

Draw or doodle about any impressions you had as you read or anything that stood out to you from this story:

Word cloud fun! Write words in the cloud that help you remember important things from this chapter:

See page 18 from the Book for an example

Date _____

Gaining a testimony of Jesus Christ changed the Lamanites.

How does having a testimony help you in every day life? _____

_____

_____

_____

_____

_____

_____

Continued on page _____

What is something Heavenly Father wants you to remember that you will

focus on this week? Write how remembering blesses you. _____

_____

_____

_____

_____

_____

Continued on page _____

What thoughts, feelings, or questions do you have from this story? _____

_____

_____

_____

_____

_____

_____

_____

_____

_____

_____

_____

_____

_____

_____

_____

_____

_____

What is your favorite scripture from this story? How does it help you? _____

_____

_____

_____

_____

_____

_____

_____

_____

_____

_____

_____

_____

MEMORIZE

Can you say the Memorize
verse when you only see
the first letter of each word?

"I_ I_ U___ T__ r___ O_ O__
r_____, W__ I_ C_____, T__
S__ O_ G__, T___ Y_ M___ B____
Y___ F_____." (HeLaMaN 5:12)

Draw or doodle about any impressions you had as you read or anything that stood out to you from this story:

Word cloud fun! Write words in the cloud that help you remember important things from this chapter:

Date _____

How can knowing that the Lord let Nephi know about

the Judge's murder help you want to repent? What have the blessings of

repenting felt like to you? _____

_____

_____

_____

_____

_____

_____

Continued on page _____

What will you start doing to help you and your family stay faithful to Jesus

Christ? Record how this affects your family. _____

_____

_____

_____

_____

_____

_____

Continued on page _____

What thoughts, feelings, or questions do you have from this story? _____

_____

_____

_____

_____

_____

_____

_____

_____

_____

_____

_____

_____

_____

_____

_____

_____

_____

_____

What is your favorite scripture from this story? How does it help you? _____

_____

_____

_____

_____

_____

_____

_____

_____

_____

_____

_____

_____

_____

_____

Can you say the Memorize
verse when you only see
the first letter of each word?

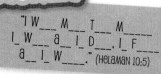

MEMORIZE

"I W___ M___ T___ M_____
I_ W___ a__ I_ D___, I_ F____
a__ I_ W____." (HeLaMaN 10:5)

Draw or doodle about any impressions you had as you read or anything that stood out to you from this story:

Word cloud fun! Write words in the cloud that help you remember important things from this chapter:

See page 18 from the Book for an example

Date _____

Are there teachings from the prophets today that are hard for you, but necessary to follow, and how have you been blessed by obedience?

_____

_____

_____

_____

_____

_____

_____

Continued on page _____

How will you prepare while you're younger to serve a mission? _____

_____

_____

_____

_____

_____

_____

_____

Continued on page _____

What thoughts, feelings, or questions do you have from this story? _____

What is your favorite scripture from this story? How does it help you? _____

_____

_____

_____

_____

_____

_____

_____

_____

_____

_____

_____

_____

_____

_____

MEMORIZE

Can you say the Memorize
verse when you only see
the first letter of each word?

"T___ C_____ T__ S__ O_ G__
T_ r_____ a__ T____ W__
S____ B_____." (Helaman 14:2)

Draw or doodle about any impressions you had as you read or anything that stood out to you from this story:

Word cloud fun! Write words in the cloud that help you remember important things from this chapter:

Date _____

How do you think the believers stayed faithful even when their lives were being threatened? _____

_____

_____

_____

_____

_____

_____

_____

Continued on page _____

What are ways you will be an example for good each day to those you are around? _____

_____

_____

_____

_____

_____

_____

Continued on page _____

What thoughts, feelings, or questions do you have from this story?

What is your favorite scripture from this story? How does it help you? _____

_____

_____

_____

_____

_____

_____

_____

_____

_____

_____

_____

_____

_____

_____

Can you say the Memorize
verse when you only see
the first letter of each word?

"B_ O_ G___ C____."
(3 NEPHI 1:13)

Draw or doodle about any impressions you had as you read or anything that stood out to you from this story:

Word cloud fun! Write words in the cloud that help you remember important things from this chapter:

See page 18 from the Book for an example.

Date _____

What can you learn about God's willingness to forgive from this story? _____

_____

_____

_____

_____

_____

_____

_____

Continued on page _____

What will you commit to do to be successful against Satan's attacks and

temptations? Write how doing this makes you feel. _____

_____

_____

_____

_____

_____

Continued on page _____

What thoughts, feelings, or questions do you have from this story? _____

_____

_____

_____

_____

_____

_____

_____

_____

_____

_____

_____

_____

_____

_____

_____

_____

_____

What is your favorite scripture from this story? How does it help you? _____

_____

_____

_____

_____

_____

_____

_____

_____

_____

_____

_____

_____

_____

_____

_____

_____

Can you say the Memorize
verse when you only see
the first letter of each word?

MEMORIZE

"C__ U___ T__
L___ F__ S_____."
(3 NEPHI 3:12)

Draw or doodle about any impressions you had as you read or anything that stood out to you from this story:

Word cloud fun! Write words in the cloud that help you remember important things from this chapter:

Date _____

Why do you think most of the people quickly went back to going against God? How can knowing this help you? _____

_____

_____

_____

_____

_____

Continued on page _____

How will you help other people know how important they are to you and to God? Write how this blesses your life. _____

_____

_____

_____

_____

_____

_____

Continued on page _____

What thoughts, feelings, or questions do you have from this story? _____

_____

_____

_____

_____

_____

_____

_____

_____

_____

_____

_____

_____

_____

_____

_____

_____

_____

_____

What is your favorite scripture from this story? How does it help you? _____

_____

_____

_____

_____

_____

_____

_____

_____

_____

_____

_____

_____

_____

_____

_____

MEMORIZE

Can you say the Memorize
verse when you only see
the first letter of each word?

"T___ W___ F___, a__ S_____.
a__ I_____. W_____ W___ a__
D_____ T_ K___ T__ C_____
O_ T__ L___." (3 NEPHI 6:14)

Draw or doodle about any impressions you had as you read or anything that stood out to you from this story:

Word cloud fun! Write words in the cloud that help you remember important things from this chapter:

See page 18 from the Book for an example

Date _____

What do you think the Lord means when he asks the people to be converted? _____

_____

_____

_____

_____

_____

_____

_____

Continued on page _____

What will you do differently to more fully have the Lord's protection? Write

how doing this affects you. _____

_____

_____

_____

_____

_____

_____

Continued on page _____

What thoughts, feelings, or questions do you have from this story? _____ _____

What is your favorite scripture from this story? How does it help you? _____

_____

_____

_____

_____

_____

_____

_____

_____

_____

_____

_____

_____

_____

_____

_____

Can you say the Memorize verse when you only see the first letter of each word?

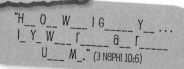

MEMORIZE

"H__ O__ W___ I G_____ Y__ . . .
I_ Y_ W___ r____ a__ r____
U___ M_." (3 NePHI 10:6)

Draw or doodle about any impressions you had as you read or anything that stood out to you from this story:

Word cloud fun! Write words in the cloud that help you remember important things from this chapter:

Date _____

How do you think you would have felt if you were there to actually feel the Savior's wounds? _____

_____

_____

_____

_____

_____

_____

_____

Continued on page _____

What will you start doing this week to become more like Jesus Christ? Write how doing this makes you feel. _____

_____

_____

_____

_____

_____

_____

Continued on page _____

What thoughts, feelings, or questions do you have from this story? _____

_____

_____

_____

_____

_____

_____

_____

_____

_____

_____

_____

_____

_____

_____

_____

_____

_____

What is your favorite scripture from this story? How does it help you? _____

_____

_____

_____

_____

_____

_____

_____

_____

_____

_____

_____

_____

_____

_____

_____

MEMORIZE

Can you say the Memorize
verse when you only see
the first letter of each word?

"T_____ I W____ T___
Y_ S_____ B_ P_____ e___ a_ I,
O_ Y___ F_____ W__ I_ I_ H_____
I_ P_____." (3 NePHI 12:48)

Draw or doodle about any impressions you had as you read or anything that stood out to you from this story:

Word cloud fun! Write words in the cloud that help you remember important things from this chapter:

See page 18 from the Book for an example.

Date _____

How does always remembering the Savior bless you in your life?

_____

_____

_____

_____

_____

_____

_____

_____

Continued on page _____

What is a goal you can make to help you become more loving like Jesus?

Write how doing this affects the people you're around. _____

_____

_____

_____

_____

_____

_____

Continued on page _____

What thoughts, feelings, or questions do you have from this story?_____

_____

_____

_____

_____

_____

_____

_____

_____

_____

_____

_____

_____

_____

_____

_____

_____

_____

_____

_____

What is your favorite scripture from this story? How does it help you? _____

_____

_____

_____

_____

_____

_____

_____

_____

_____

_____

_____

_____

_____

_____

MEMORIZE

Can you say the Memorize
verse when you only see
the first letter of each word?

"W_____ Y_ S____ a__
T__ F____ I_ M_ N___. W____
I_ T____, B_____ T___ Y_ S____
T_____, B_____ I_ S___ B_ G____
U___ Y__." (3 NEPHI 18:20)

Draw or doodle about any impressions you had as you read or anything that stood out to you from this story:

Word cloud fun! Write words in the cloud that help you remember important things from this chapter:

Date _____

How do you feel when you reverently take the sacrament? _____

_____

_____

_____

_____

_____

_____

_____

Continued on page _____

Write what you will do to become better at recognizing the influence of the

Spirit. Share how doing this blesses you. _____

_____

_____

_____

_____

_____

_____

_____

Continued on page _____

What thoughts, feelings, or questions do you have from this story?_____

_____

_____

_____

_____

_____

_____

_____

_____

_____

_____

_____

_____

_____

_____

_____

_____

_____

What is your favorite scripture from this story? How does it help you? _____

_____

_____

_____

_____

_____

_____

_____

_____

_____

_____

_____

_____

_____

_____

_____

MEMORIZE

Can you say the Memorize verse when you only see the first letter of each word?

"T__ W____ W____ Y_ H___ S___ M_ D_ T___ S____ Y_ a___ D_." (3 NEPHI 27:21)

Draw or doodle about any impressions you had as you read or anything that stood out to you from this story:

Word cloud fun! Write words in the cloud that help you remember important things from this chapter:

See page 18 from the Book for an example

Date _____

What can you do to love sharing the gospel like the disciples

did? _____

_____

_____

_____

_____

_____

_____

_____

Continued on page _____

What will you do to make choices that Jesus would feel are good too? Write

how this helps you. _____

_____

_____

_____

_____

_____

Continued on page _____

What thoughts, feelings, or questions do you have from this story? _____

_____

_____

_____

_____

_____

_____

_____

_____

_____

_____

_____

_____

_____

_____

_____

_____

What is your favorite scripture from this story? How does it help you? _____

_____

_____

_____

_____

_____

_____

_____

_____

_____

_____

_____

_____

_____

_____

MEMORIZE

Can you say the Memorize
verse when you only see
the first letter of each word?

"Y_ S_____ S__ D___ I_ T_
K_____ O_ M_ F_____; Y__, Y___
J__ S____ B_ F___. . . . a__ Y_ S____
B_ e___ a_ I a_." (3 NEPHI 28:10)

Draw or doodle about any impressions you had as you read or anything that stood out to you from this story:

Word cloud fun! Write words in the cloud that help you remember important things from this chapter:

Date _____

Why do you think the people would have chosen to do things that stopped them from being peaceful and happy? How has obeying a commandment made you happy? _____

_____

_____

_____

_____

_____

Continued on page _____

What will you do differently to show more love to others like Jesus taught?

_____

_____

_____

_____

_____

_____

_____

Continued on page _____

What thoughts, feelings, or questions do you have from this story? _____

_____

_____

_____

_____

_____

_____

_____

_____

_____

_____

_____

_____

_____

_____

_____

_____

_____

What is your favorite scripture from this story? How does it help you? _____

_____

_____

_____

_____

_____

_____

_____

_____

_____

_____

_____

_____

_____

Can you say the Memorize
verse when you only see
the first letter of each word?

MEMORIZE

"T___ W__ N_ C_____
...B_____ O_ T__ L___ O_ G__
W____ D__ D____ I_ T__ H_____
O_ T__ P_____." (4 NEPHI 1:15)

Draw or doodle about any impressions you had as you read or anything that stood out to you from this story:

Word cloud fun! Write words in the cloud that help you remember important things from this chapter:

Date _____

What kinds of important things (like working hard on your

education) do young Mormon's experiences inspire you to do? _____

_____

_____

_____

_____

_____

_____

_____

Continued on page _____

What will you commit to do to help you live righteously, like Mormon, even

if others are not? _____

_____

_____

_____

_____

_____

_____

Continued on page _____

What thoughts, feelings, or questions do you have from this story?_____

_____

_____

_____

_____

_____

_____

_____

_____

_____

_____

_____

_____

_____

_____

_____

_____

What is your favorite scripture from this story? How does it help you? _____

_____

_____

_____

_____

_____

_____

_____

_____

_____

_____

_____

_____

_____

MEMORIZE

Can you say the Memorize verse when you only see the first letter of each word?

"C___ U___ J____ W___ B_____ H_____ a__ c_____ S_____." (MORMON 2:14)

Draw or doodle about any impressions you had as you read or anything that stood out to you from this story:

Word cloud fun! Write words in the cloud that help you remember important things from this chapter:

Date _____

How can the examples of Mormon and Moroni help you to be your very best throughout your whole life? _____

_____

_____

_____

_____

_____

_____

_____

Continued on page _____

What will you do to be confident and humble at the same time? Write how doing this makes you feel. _____

_____

_____

_____

_____

_____

_____

Continued on page _____

What thoughts, feelings, or questions do you have from this story?

What is your favorite scripture from this story? How does it help you? _____

MEMORIZE

Can you say the Memorize verse when you only see the first letter of each word?

"W____ B_____ I_ C_____.
D_____ N_____. W_____
H_ S___ a__ T__ F_____ I_T_
N__ O_ C_____ I_ S____ B_
G_____ H__." (MORMON 9:21)

Draw or doodle about any impressions you had as you read or anything that stood out to you from this story:

Word cloud fun! Write words in the cloud that help you remember important things from this chapter:

See page 18 from the Book for an example

Date _____

What impresses you about the prayers of the Brother of Jared?

_____

_____

_____

_____

_____

_____

Continued on page _____

What choices will you make to strengthen your faith to be like the Brother

of Jared's? Record how doing these blesses your life. _____

_____

_____

_____

_____

_____

_____

_____

Continued on page _____

What thoughts, feelings, or questions do you have from this story? _____

What is your favorite scripture from this story? How does it help you? _____

_____

_____

_____

_____

_____

_____

_____

_____

_____

_____

_____

_____

_____

_____

_____

Can you say the Memorize verse when you only see the first letter of each word?

MEMORIZE

"W___ H_____ B_____ T__ L___."
(ETHEr 6:30)

Draw or doodle about any impressions you had as you read or anything that stood out to you from this story:

Word cloud fun! Write words in the cloud that help you remember important things from this chapter:

Date _____

Why do think the Jaredites wouldn't just stop fighting and
repent, and how can this help you to not argue or fight? _____

_____

_____

_____

_____

_____

_____

Continued on page _____

What will you do each day to help you remember God and His love for you?

_____

_____

_____

_____

_____

_____

_____

Continued on page _____

What thoughts, feelings, or questions do you have from this story?_____

_____

_____

_____

_____

_____

_____

_____

_____

_____

_____

_____

_____

_____

_____

_____

_____

What is your favorite scripture from this story? How does it help you? _____

_____

_____

_____

_____

_____

_____

_____

_____

_____

_____

_____

_____

_____

_____

Can you say the Memorize
verse when you only see
the first letter of each word?

MEMORIZE

"Y_ r_____ N_ W_____ U___
a____ T__ T____ O_ Y___ F____."
(ETHer 12:6)

Draw or doodle about any impressions you had as you read or anything that stood out to you from this story:

Word cloud fun! Write words in the cloud that help you remember important things from this chapter:

See page 18 from the Book for an example

Date _____

How can you develop spiritual strength and a testimony like

Moroni? _____

_____

_____

_____

_____

_____

_____

Continued on page _____

What can you do to be more like Jesus Christ today? Write how being more

like Jesus blesses your life. _____

_____

_____

_____

_____

_____

Continued on page _____

What thoughts, feelings, or questions do you have from this story?_____

_____

_____

_____

_____

_____

_____

_____

_____

_____

_____

_____

_____

_____

_____

_____

_____

_____

_____

What is your favorite scripture from this story? How does it help you? _____

_____

_____

_____

_____

_____

_____

_____

_____

_____

_____

_____

_____

_____

_____

_____

Can you say the Memorize
verse when you only see
the first letter of each word?

MEMORIZE

"B_ T__ P____ O_ T__ H___ G____
Y_ M__ K___ T__ T____ O_ a__
T_____." (MOroNI 10:5)

Draw or doodle about any impressions you had as you read or anything that stood out to you from this story:

Word cloud fun! Write words in the cloud that help you remember important things from this chapter:

Continued writing from page _____

Continued writing from page _____

Continued writing from page _____

Continued writing from page _____

_____

_____

_____

_____

_____

_____

_____

_____

_____

_____

_____

_____

_____

_____

_____

_____

_____

_____

_____

_____

Continued writing from page _____

Continued writing from page _____

Continued writing from page _____

Continued writing from page _____

Continued writing from page _____

Continued writing from page _____

Continued writing from page _____

Continued writing from page _____